HERBS
from a
NORFOLK KITCHEN

by
CARLA PHILLIPS

Additional recipes from
NORFOLK LAVENDER

Contents

Contents

NOTE

Throughout the book, where "tablespoons" have been used in the ingredients, if accuracy is crucial, American, Imperial or Continental have been differentiated.

American and Imperial teaspoons are identical.

3 teaspoons = 1 American tablespoon.

4 teaspoons = 1 Imperial or Continental tablespoon.

Introduction

There is an old Russian folk tale about how salt was brought to a faraway kingdom, The king, his courtiers and subjects, previously listless, depressed and dispirited, found their lives and dispositions immeasurably enriched. They lavishly rewarded the giver.

This is what flavouring does; the secret of many a famed 'plain cook' is the liberal use of a pepper mill.

Unlike most spices, which come from exotic and distant places, herbs come to hand easily. They can be grown in city window boxes, take up small patches of garden, or can be bought, fresh and green, in many supermarkets. Dried, they are available in most corner shops. They have specific medicinal benefits, which I won't go into. But, most of all, they add that extra twist of taste which makes an ordinary dish delicious.

There are pitfalls in using herbs. If they are too old, have no aroma left, smell musty - they must be jettisoned. Too many strong herbs put together may battle each other. But, using herbs is the most effective way of improving the most basic sort of cookery. Try and see what a difference a bay leaf or two in the water will make, when you're cooking potatoes. See what a sprinkling of a small amount of thyme will do to a chop, lamb or pork. Or, chop a handful of fresh parsley over the most simple salad, or a piece of steamed or baked fish.

I was not trained as a cook. As I struggled to feed a large family, without great amounts of money, I learnt from friends, relations, books. Our little herb garden was immediately outside our kitchen door, so that even in snow, I could quickly locate and pull up a sprig or two of parsley, a scrap of rosemary or sage. Years further on, after working in a busy restaurant with no garden at all, I still miss that convenient little herb patch. Even though most fresh herbs are now easily available, I still have several pots of basil growing on all available window sills, come summer time.

Some of the recipes in this book are those which used to feed family and friends. Some have developed since, feeding the growing crowds of good friends who started out simply as restaurant customers.

We started our restaurant in a small seaside town on the North Norfolk coast, fifty yards away from the quay. From the start, we concentrated on finding, buying and cooking food from our immediate area. Fish and game from the shore and woods. Local vegetables, abundant all year round. If it was an exotic based ingredient, from a few continents away, a different ocean – we didn't bother, preferring to concentrate on local riches. This doesn't mean that we dispensed with the great range of condiments and flavourings now available to most serious cooks. But herbs remain a main stay.

There are very very few traditional recipes left in our region. From the enclosing of pastureland to the industrial revolution and the dispersal of large rural populations to the cities, domestic traditions were severely assaulted, demolishing what had once been a rich culinary culture. I feel that the nearest links to the traditional cookery of East Anglia are the old New England recipes, brought over by ship loads of emigrating East Anglians in the 17th and 18th centuries.

I have tried to give instructions in measurements understood by English, American, and metric cooks. But, when it comes to the actual fine touching of flavours, all recipes can be tweaked and adjusted to suit the state of the ingredients at hand as well as the temperament of the individual cook.

A final word of warning; don't overdose your dishes with herbs. Too much, particularly when you're using the more strongly flavoured sage, rosemary or lavender, and you will obliterate all other flavours. The texture of your dishes, when you're using the whole herb, must be remembered. I've watched diners spit out and pick out twigs and branches of rosemary and bay as they tried to eat. Parsley stalks, wonderful for flavouring stocks and sauces, taste like string if left in when serving the final product.

I've concentrated on savoury cooking with herbs because the flavours of herbs match that side of cookery so very well. With the exception of mint, and to a lesser extent lavender, puddings with herbs are not too successful a marriage.

COLD SAUCES

The cold sauces which start this collection of recipes are very useful – not only for the salads suggested, but with cold cooked vegetables, and, at a pinch, with hot plainly cooked vegetables or fish. Vinaigrette and a few simply microwaved vegetables can be a quick saviour on a busy night!

Parsley and Mustard Vinaigrette

INGREDIENTS:

The juice of 2 lemons

30 ml of Dijon mustard
(1 fl.oz : 2 Am. tablespoons)

2 cloves of garlic, peeled, with, in winter, the green central pith extracted

2 shallots

A good handful of fresh parsley

300 ml of sunflower oil
(at least $^1/_2$ pint : $1^1/_4$ cups)

This is what I serve with most green salads. If all the ingredients (particularly the oil) are at room temperature, and it is made slowly and carefully, the result is a thick and emulsified sauce which wonderfully accompanies the simplest of salad leaves. I am giving good sized quantities for it as it will stay very well at room temperature, for four of five days (there being nothing to spoil in it).

METHOD

In the bowl of a food processor or blender mix together the garlic, shallots, mustard, parsley and lemon juice. Gradually, very gradually, trickle in the sunflower oil, pausing occasionally to ensure that the mixture is thickening.

For a variation or two, you can add a few drops of Worcestershire sauce or Soy sauce. The Worcestershire is particularly nice if you've added a few chunks of cheese to your salad, and the Soy sauce is good if there are some bean sprouts and Chinese leaves among the lettuce leaves.

Shallot Vinaigrette

INGREDIENTS:

2 or 3 shallots

2 tablespoons of sherry
vinegar

1 teaspoon of dried thyme

Black pepper, freshly
milled

300 ml of light vegetable
oil – grapeseed or
sunflower.
(At least 1/2 pint : 1 1/4 cups)

This is a useful dressing for shellfish – great with cockles, and also with their American cousins, clams. I've seen it served with freshly opened oysters, but honestly wouldn't recommend it – it's too strong for the delicate taste of oysters. It keeps well out of the refrigerator, and can be poured into a narrow necked bottle, to be shaken out, when needed.

METHOD

Using a food processor or blender, mince the shallot with the sherry vinegar, pepper and thyme. Starting slowly, dribble in a stream the oil into the rest of the ingredients. I wouldn't add salt if you're using this with seafood, which already contains quite a bit of salt.

Mustard, Herb and Caper Sauce

INGREDIENTS:

2 small shallots

2 hard boiled eggs

1 normal (raw) egg

30 ml Dijon mustard
(1 fl.oz : 2 Am. tablespoons)
the same amount of capers

A handful of tarragon
leaves
(2 teaspoons of freeze dried
tarragon leaves)

A handful of fresh parsley

A few sprigs of dill

30 ml of cider vinegar
(1 fl.oz : 2 Am. tablespoons)

A handful of chervil
(if available)

360 ml of sunflower oil
(12 fl.oz : 1^{1}/2 cups)

A couple of teaspoons of
hot water

For a garnish: capers and
parsley

This is particularly wonderful with tongue. Either cold cooked tongue, sliced thinly, or thickly sliced tongue, served hot by grilling on both sides on one of those heavy ridged grill pans used on top of your stove. But, if you're not a fan of tongue, this sauce is super as a luncheon salad dressing for a mixture of green leaves, tomatoes and sliced avocados.

METHOD

In the bowl of a processor or blender combine the hard boiled egg yolks with the yolk of the uncooked egg, the vinegar, mustard, herbs and shallots and capers. Mix well, then add the oil, dribbling it in, mayonnaise fashion. Last of all the cooked egg whites, and when they are blended in, add a little hot water to thin slightly. A nice garnish is more capers and a little chopped parsley.

Mustard and Dill Sauce

INGREDIENTS:

30 ml of Dijon mustard
(1 fl.oz : 2 Am. tablespoons)

3 teaspoons of sugar

A handful of fresh dill or
a tablespoon of freeze
dried dill

1 teaspoon of dried
mustard

1 large or 2 small shallots

30 ml of cider vinegar
(1 oz : 2 Am tablespoons)

300 ml of sunflower oil
($^1/_2$ pint : $1^1/_4$ cups)

A little hot water.

Served with pickled fish, such as gravlax, this is also well suited to cold cooked meat, particularly ham, and cold cooked bacon joints. Its sweet and sour flavours marry well with some smoked fish as well.

METHOD

In a blender or processor mix together the mustard, sugar, dill, vinegar and shallot(s). Gradually blend in the oil. Last of all add the water which will lighten and thin the sauce so that it will pour rather than require ladling. If you wish, you can add more sugar – but this depends on how salty the meat or fish is (which the sauce is supposed to accompany), as well as how sweet a tooth you may have!

The ideal garnish for this is a sprig or two of fresh dill.

Dill

Cumin and Coriander Sauce

INGREDIENTS:

A teacupful (more or less) of mayonnaise. At a pinch, you can use a commercial type, but homemade is best

$1/2$ red pepper, with the seeds removed and the inside white core cut out

1 small chilli, deseeded and cored (Make sure that you rinse your hands well after handling!)

The juice of a lime

A handful of coriander (fresh)

2 level teaspoons of cumin

60 ml of olive oil
(2 fl.oz : 4 Am. tablespoons)

This is one of the best accompaniments I know of for "posh" fish, whether steamed or fried. Particularly good with prawns, scampi or monkfish, this sauce is also a nice accompaniment to a couple of hard boiled eggs, with summery, salad accompaniments: cold peeled broad beans; cold French beans; tomatoes; new potatoes. While the ingredients, used in larger quantities, are often found in fierce and colourful sauces, when combined in this mayonnaise based sauce, they are gentle, subtle and in tune with the ingredients they are supposed to accompany.

Cumin

METHOD

In a blender or food processor, mix together the mayonnaise with the pepper, lime juice, chilli, coriander and cumin. Make sure that they are well blended before dribbling in, very slowly, the olive oil.

Garlic and Parsley Mayonnaise

INGREDIENTS:

The juice of 1 lemon

2 egg yolks

2 large or 3 – 4 small
cloves of garlic

1 shallot

3 teaspoons of Dijon
mustard
($^1/_2$ fl.oz : 1 Am. tablespoon)

300 ml of Sunflower oil
($^1/_2$ pint : 1$^1/_4$ cups)

A generous handful of
parsley, stalks removed

This is versatile. Good in a fish soup, even a bought or tinned one. Nice with smoked chicken or seafood. Fine as a dip with finely sliced celery sticks, carrots, cherry tomatoes, or sprigs of cauliflower. Even tasty with fried fish or fish fingers!

METHOD

In a blender or food processor, mix together the egg yolks, lemon juice, garlic, parsley, mustard, shallot. Dribble in, very gradually, the oil.

Try to make sure that both the egg yolks and oil are at room temperature before you start in order to eliminate all chances of separation.

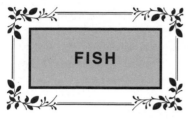

FISH

I haven't differentiated too much when I gave recipes for fish. I'm not convinced that cooked salmon, sea trout or large river trout are that different – and anyway, feel that sauces for them require more spice than herbs. Flatfish, whether flounder, dabs, brill or sole are best simply treated, and I prefer them either steamed or pan fried (dipped in milk, then in flour seasoned with salt and pepper and then fried briefly in either sunflower oil or clarified butter). Then, they can be accompanied by either a light sauce or butter. The one exception I would make to all this is the shark family – known as rock salmon, huss, tope, dogfish – which if fresh and skinned, is meaty and juicy and more reminiscent of chicken or rabbit and able to stand up to a more robust type of cookery.

Fish Cookery with Herbs
Steamed Fish over Lavender

I don't think that this section of the book can contain too many hard and fast recipes. Fish come in all sorts of varieties and sizes, depending on where they're caught and how – which makes a general recipe completely unsuitable. Freshness is all, and the least amount of handling is best. A day old sole or flounder, a fresh dab – nicely trimmed (Be ruthless! Cut away those outer bones and save them for stock!) – then dipped quickly in milk, and seasoned flour, and fried quickly in either a light oil or clarified butter – needs little else. Or, a larger flat fish, such as halibut or turbot, or one of the grander "round" fish, such as sea bass – either filleted or cut into a steak – can be brushed with a little oil and baked in foil. Or, quickest, and I think best, these fish, or fillets or steaks, can be briefly steamed, on a rack over water which is salted and strewn with a good teaspoon of dried lavender. Dust the fish lightly with a small amount of parsley, and steam until the fish starts to change from translucent to opaque. Turn off the heat, cover, and leave the fish to finish cooking in the ambient steam remaining. Perfection.

Marinade for the Shark Family

INGREDIENTS:

2 limes

1 chilli, de-seeded, and with its inner ribs pared away (wash your hands after doing this!)

2 shallots

A handful of fresh coriander

A dash of salt and black pepper

A tablespoon of olive oil

If you find a really fresh piece of one of the shark family: dogfish, huss, tope, "rock salmon", it is worthwhile filleting it – by turning it round, and with a sharp knife removing the central cartilaginous bone throughout the centre, scraping away the dark "blood" that surrounds this. Easily tackled and accomplished with a smallish sharp knife! You will be left with a very long strip of filleted fish which you can cut into serving sized steaks. These are terrific if marinated for several hours, or even overnight in the following marinade.

METHOD

Roughly zest the lime. Add this and the juice of the limes to the rest of the ingredients and blend or process them together. Rub them well over the fish fillets, place them in a glass or pottery dish (or a non-reactive stainless bowl), cover and refrigerate for up to ten hours. To cook the marinaded fish, either barbecue it out of doors, which is really the best way, or lay it on a very hot ridged cast iron grill, which has been brushed with a little oil. It will cook in minutes – and you can tell it's cooked, if a knife or fork easily go through the thickest portion of flesh.

This fish dish is fine eaten as it is, accompanied by summer type vegetables: peppers, tomatoes, courgettes, aubergines, etc. But if you really want a little sauce for it, to further gild the lily, this little dipping sauce, simply and quickly made suits it to perfection.

Dipping Sauce for the Shark Family

INGREDIENTS:

2 tablespoons of mayonnaise

Juice of 1 lime

2 teaspoons of Dijon mustard

A few chopped leaves of coriander

A few drops of Worcestershire sauce

There is no need to be too precise about this particular sauce. Invented when there wasn't a lot of anything else around, there are no fixed quantities.

METHOD

Mix all together to taste. Dab rather than dollop this sauce next to servings of fish.

Coriander

Red Wine and Lavender Butter for Fried Fish

INGREDIENTS:

3 shallots, chopped

A handful of parsley

2 teaspoons of dried lavender

A bottle of red wine

A tablespoon of Balsamic vinegar

A good dash of freshly ground pepper

A teaspoon of salt

600 gm of unsalted butter (1 1/4 lb)

This looks like a suspicious dollop of pink yogurt or ice cream at first, when served with a fried fillet of fish. As it melts, it is an easy and delicious accompaniment to an otherwise simple meal. It's best made in a large quantity, then rolled into long circular bars, and refrigerated – it will last for a month or two in a fridge, longer in a freezer.

METHOD

Place the shallots, lavender, parsley and red wine in a saucepan and boil them together until they have reduced to a couple of tablespoons of fluid. Add the salt, pepper and vinegar and return to the boil. Then remove from the fire and place in a food processor. Gradually beat in the butter. At first it will be a red liquid, and then you will have a pink and fluffy substance. Dollop it in large spoonfuls onto some silicone or greaseproof paper and roll it into long bars, which you can place on a tray. When it is completely chilled and firm you'll be able to handle the rolled up bars individually, for storage. If it is too liquid to be easily rolled into long bars, chill the entire mixture briefly – about a quarter of an hour, and it will be simple to handle.

To serve, cut a coin or two off the long bar and place these on top of the fried fish immediately before the plate is handed out. This butter is also very tasty placed on a simple piece of steamed fish.

Mint, Soy and Garlic Vinaigrette

INGREDIENTS:

2 – 3 cloves of garlic,
peeled and crushed

2 tablespoons of Tamari
soy sauce

2 tablespoons of Thai or
Vietnamese fish sauce
(Nam Pla or Nuoc Mam)

2 tablespoons of
red wine vineger

1 teaspoon of Chinese
chilli sauce

A few drops of Tabasco

A generous handful
(at least) of fresh mint,
finely chopped

4 tablespoons of
sunflower oil

This is one of those orientally inspired sauces which seem to match with fish, whether steamed, fried or made into fish cakes or croquettes. It has a fairly strong and intense taste, which means that it shouldn't douse whatever it's meant to accompany.

METHOD

Combine all these ingredients together in a jar with a cover, and leave to stand for at least a half hour in the refrigerator, before shaking up, then serving, in small amounts, spooned lightly over the fish or fish cakes.

Mint

Fish Cakes

INGREDIENTS:

The cooked and flaked fish

1 small onion or two shallots, finely minced

1 large blade of celery, finely minced

Either half a large green pepper or a small green pepper, finely minced

1 egg

A heaped tablespoon of mayonnaise

A large handful of parsley, finely chopped

Salt and pepper

Cayenne

At least 2 oz of breadcrumbs

More breadcrumbs for rolling the cakes in

Oil or oil and butter for frying

This is the type of recipe that any cook with a mania for precise instruction is not going to warm to. Fish cakes are a popular dish with just about anyone. They carry no risk of bones and have the comforting texture of a crisp exterior as well as the promise of a little seasoning or spice to relieve the often bland taste of plain fish. They can also be made from almost any cooked fish imaginable whether it is finely textured, like salmon or flounder, or coarsely flaked like cod and members of the cod family. The fish cakes can be titivated further by adding a little crab or chopped up shrimp or prawn, in order to make them slightly fancier.

Parsley

The English habit is to mix cooked fish with mashed potato, but I don't like this combination. It tends to make fishcakes into a heavy meal. I prefer breadcrumbs, which lighten the texture considerably, especially if they are soft, day old breadcrumbs as opposed to the dried out dusty things sold ready-made in packets. Cracker meal, or crushed up water biscuits, will also give a light texture to the finished product.

But, and this is important, the amount to use cannot be given too categorically. Some fish is 'wetter' than others when cooked. Some fish is flakier. Some people are more deft at ladling a slightly sloppy batter then other folks. You can plan to use no more than a couple of ounces, which is about a half cupful of breadcrumbs for three quarters of a pound of cooked fish. But if it is too difficult to handle, try adding a little more crumb, until you can form it into a cake or croquette. Then chill it well.

So, for three quarters of a pound of cooked fish, which should feed four or five people, you will need

METHOD

Combine the onion, celery and green pepper with the egg and mayonnaise. Mix them well, then add the flaked fish and the parsley. Add the seasoning, with a light hand for the salt, and a good sprinkling of pepper and cayenne. Last of all, gradually add the breadcrumbs, mixing it until the texture is just firm enough to form into cakes or balls. Chill the cakes until you are ready to cook them.

When you are ready to cook them, heat a large, heavy-bottomed frying pan, then add a little oil, and finally, if you like, a little butter. Place the fish cakes in the heated fat, leaving them until they are quite brown underneath, before flipping them over. Frequent turning of them will only make them disintegrate to a point where you will have to practice fish cake sculpture.

They can be served as they are, with just a twist of lemon, or can be accompanied by either a mayonnaise spiked with a few herbs and gherkins and the juice of a lemon, or another sauce of your choice, including Mint, Soy and Garlic Vinaigrette. A sprinkle or two of fresh parsley is always a good idea.

VEGETABLES

Whether it's the bay leaf in the salt water you use for potatoes, or the marjoram and oregano sprinkled over tomatoes, or the parsley over anything and everything, it is easy to combine vegetables and herbs. They have perfect affinities and there are very few vegetables which don't combine well with at least one herb.

Stronger herbs can often be substituted for each other. A little lavender can be used in place of rosemary – or vice versa. but don't try to combine the stronger herbs, otherwise you'll have a final dish which is redolent of these herbs, but of very little else.

Chives

Rosemary Potatoes

INGREDIENTS:

1 kg of potatoes
(a generous 2 lbs)

45 mm of olive oil
(1¹/₂ fl.oz : 3 Am.
tablespoons)

**2 cloves of garlic, finely
minced**

**Very finely chopped green
sprigs of one fresh
rosemary branch**

Salt and pepper

Coarse sea salt

Rosemary

This recipe, which serves four generously, is useful just when the new potato crop has come to an end, and before main crop potatoes are available. In other words, just when the potatoes are too firm when cooked to be mashed or crumbly, but not quite tasty enough on their own to be served as new potatoes.

METHOD

Put a large saucepan of water containing a couple of teaspoons of salt on to boil. then scrub and finely slice the potatoes. It isn't necessary to peel them.

When the water reaches a full boil, slide the potatoes in. When it returns to a fierce boil drain the potatoes thoroughly in a colander. With a little of the olive oil, lightly oil a large Pyrex baking dish, roasting tin or casserole. Then, in a large mixing bowl mix together the rest of the oil, the garlic, rosemary and some salt and pepper. Mix the potatoes into this, tossing them well in order to oil most of the layers, then place them in the baking dish. Dot with a trickle or two of olive oil, then sprinkle them lightly with coarse sea salt. Bake them in a hot oven for thirty to forty minutes, or until crisp on top. You can lower the temperature and leave them for a little while after that.

Good with plain meat or fish.

Cauliflower and Calabrese with Mustard and Tarragon Sauce

INGREDIENTS:

225 ml of cream
(8 fl.oz)

30 ml of Dijon mustard
(1 fl.oz : 2 Am. tablespoons)

Juice of 1/2 lemon

A few strips of red pepper,
finely chopped (about a
quarter of an average red
pepper)

Several leaves of fresh
tarragon, finely chopped up

Cauli, broccoli, sprouting broccoli, romanesco, calabrese – even Brussels sprouts – all vegetables which are absolutely sweet and delicious if not over-cooked. The only way to avoid this, I have found, over years of practice, is to prepare them well, then plunge them into a very large amount of boiling, salted water. When they are just tender enough, they must be hoiked out of the water rapidly, then plunged directly into a cold bath of water, and then, when cooled, drained thoroughly.

Then they can be re-warmed – either in a tightly covered casserole which has been buttered, with a butter paper to cover the vegetables, or in a microwave oven. Good results each time!

There are a few things to remember when preparing them, however. For instance, the stems of broccoli are as delicious and tender as the flowers of the plant. To prepare them, cut off the florets and peel the tough outer skins of the stalks away. This may seem fiddly, but it seems absurd to waste so much of such a tasty vegetable.

And, unless you actually like soggy Brussels sprouts, don't worry about cutting a cross in the bottom of each sprout. This only makes the interior of the sprout soggy and overcooked. Cut away any grubby outer leaves and a bit of the stem if it seems quite tough – but that is all that is necessary. When testing the boiling sprout for doneness, use an ordinary fork to pierce the sprout to see if it is tender. Then, plunging the sprouts into cold water will stop the outer layers from disintegrating, while the hearts of the sprouts will continue to cook for a very little while, regardless.

Here is a sauce which will bring out the best in all these brassicas, as well as being a suitable match for some simply steamed fish and boiled poatatoes.

METHOD
Combine these ingredients and bring to the boil. Then place in a double saucepan, over hot water, until ready for use.

Tarragon

Leeks with Red Wine, Oregano, Tomatoes and Olive Puree

INGREDIENTS:
SERVES 4

4 leeks, well cleaned and cut into largish chunks

45 ml of Tomato Passata (chunky tomato puree)
(2 imp. tablespoons : 3 Am. tablespoons)

45 ml of red wine
(2 imp. tablespoons : 3 Am. tablespoons)

1 (scant) teaspoon of oregano

Freshly milled black pepper

2 teaspoons of black olive puree

1 tablespoon olive oil

Leeks, carefully cleaned by slitting the green tops until no dirt is visible, then riffling them well, as one shuffles a pack of cards, under a running tap – then cut into largish chunks and steamed over lightly salted boiling water with a couple of bay leaves in it, are tender, still green. Boiling leeks whole sometimes, – well, more than sometimes – results in tough, watery, grey and tasteless vegetables. If, while the steamed leeks are still warm, they are dressed with the Parsley and Mustard Vinaigrette sauce, given earlier, then allowed to chill, they make a perfect starter to a meal which features roast meat or steak or chops.

In our restaurant, however, cooking leeks with red wine and tomatoes, flavoured with oregano and olive puree, makes them a dish in their own right. Redolent of the Mediterranean, of summertime, of heat, they make a fine winter accompaniment to a simply prepared omelette or rice dish as well as a star partner for some plain fish.

METHOD
Heat a heavy saucepan, and add the olive oil. Toss the leeks around well in this until they are just starting to soften. Add the oregano and pepper and cook for another minute or two. Then add the tomato puree and the wine. Reduce the heat and allow the leeks to cook until they are done. Piercing them easily with a knife is the way to test them. Last of all, add the olive puree and mix well. Raise the heat while you stir them, and then turn it off, allowing it all to cool very slightly before serving.

Courgettes with Fennel Seeds and Lemon

INGREDIENTS:
SERVES 4 – 6

450 gm courgettes
(1 lb)

1 heaped teaspoon of
fennel seeds

1 clove of garlic, crushed

1 tablespoon of olive oil

Juice of 1 lemon

Salt and pepper

A versatile vegetable – courgettes are particularly delectable when small. Largish courgettes can be grated, salted, placed in a colander with a plate or bowl to weigh them down, and when the mixture is drained (about an hour or two), mixed with flour, an egg or two, and either chopped mint or chopped marjoram, and used then to make a sort of pancake to be sauteed in oil. Covered with a little grated cheese and some hot tomato sauce, this will make an acceptable starter or light supper dish.

But, if you wish to serve courgettes as is, in a pleasant combination, very good hot but equally acceptable cold – here is a suggestion.

METHOD

For a little visual interest, peel away along the length some of the dark skin of the courgettes, so that they have a stripey appearance. Slice into thickish (1/2 inch or centimetre sized) rounds, sprinkle with a little salt, place in a colander, cover with a plate, and leave for about a half hour. They should disgorge a little water (not very much if they are young and fresh).

When ready to cook, heat up a heavy bottomed frying pan and add the olive oil. When this is quite hot, add the courgettes and then the fennel seeds. Mix well, and cook for three or four minutes, until the courgettes are hot and tender. Then add the garlic, some black pepper, and the lemon juice, stirring well, so that the flavour is spread throughout. Leave for a further minute to cook, then cover the pan, turn off the heat and allow them to "rest" briefly before serving.

Parsley Carrots

INGREDIENTS:

450 gm of carrots
(11b)

60 gm of sugar
(2oz : $^1/_4$ cup)

60 gm of butter
(2 oz : $^1/_2$ stick)

**2 handfuls of parsley,
finely chopped**

$^1/_2$ teaspoon of salt

Freshly milled black pepper

A dash of cayenne

A rich and delicious dish, this version of Carottes Vichy will often convert previous haters of cooked carrots to fans. Absolutely beautiful with something delicate but classic such as a fish pie or a plain roasted chicken, and a good addition at feast time, such as Christmas.

METHOD

Peel and cut the carrots into smallish chunks. If the carrots are large, you may have to cut them down their length as well as chop them across. You want to arrive at nuggets, all more or less the same size, so that they all cook at the same time.

You must have a heavy bottomed saucepan for this dish, with a tight fitting cover. Heat the saucepan and add the butter. When it is melted and just beginning to bubble a little add the carrots, and turn them in the butter in order to cover them all over. Raise the heat and add the sugar continuing to stir, until they are all covered. Now add half the parsley, the salt, and enough water to cover the carrots only half way. Give them all a stir, reduce the heat and cover, to cook for five or six minutes. Then uncover, and if all the water is evaporated, and the carrots are not tender, add a little more water. When they are fork tender, add the rest of the parsley, some pepper and cayenne, switch off the heat and cover them, allowing them to finish cooking and to absorb all the flavours.

New Potatoes with Mint Butter

INGREDIENTS:

225 gm unsalted butter
($1/2$ lb)

1 shallot

$1/2$ teaspoon of salt

**A generous handful of
mint leaves**

**1 heaped teaspoon of
caster sugar**

Juice of $1/2$ lemon

**Dash of white finely
ground pepper**

New potatoes with mint, a heavensent partnership. If the potatoes are very very fresh, and the mint instantly pulled from the garden, this is the food of the Gods!

For this dish – rather, for the potato part of it, there are no set quantities. I prefer to cook the new potatoes in a steamer over water which has salt and a branch or two of mint in it. then, to gild the lily completely, I serve them with a coin or two of the following butter.

METHOD

The butter must be at room temperature for this. In a food processor, mix together the mint, sugar, lemon, salt and shallot. Then add the butter and when it is a complete, greenish mixture, dollop and dab it onto greaseproof or silicone paper, which you will roll up and chill, in bars.

Cut a coin or two onto the freshly prepared new potatoes, before serving, and garnish with a little finely shredded mint leaf.

Mint

Broad Beans with Savory and Cream

INGREDIENTS:

A good stalk or 2 of Savory

Double or whipping cream

Salt and pepper

Savory

All beans go well with savory. A good stalk or two with some leaves in the saucepan of boiling, salted water, and an incredible difference in the results – no matter which bean (broad, runner, string) you're cooking.

METHOD

Broad beans, if very fresh, and not oversized, are perhaps the best of all. Shell them, and tip them into a lot of boiling unsalted water, with a savory branch or two. Allow them to return to the boil, and then after two minutes, start to try them, to see if they are tender. They should cook in anything from three to five minutes – no more. Allow them to cook longer and they will be floury and tasteless.

When just tender and tasty, drain them and rinse them well in some cold running water. Or immerse the colander into a full basin of cold water. Then heat, in a small saucepan, some double or whipping cream, with a little more chopped savoury. Add the broad beans and salt and pepper to taste. When heated, serve immediately.

Hoi Sin, Garlic and Coriander Sauce for Cauliflower and Calabrese

INGREDIENTS:

60 ml of Hoi Sin Sauce
(2 fl.oz : 4 Am. tablespoons)

1 clove of garlic, crushed

1 tablespoon of wine
vinegar

1 pimento or red pepper,
de-seeded and de-cored

4 tablespoons of olive oil

**A handful of
fresh coriander**

Another sauce for brassicas. This one needs no cooking, and doesn't require refrigeration. Also, if you cook some pasta at the same time as the broccoli, cauli, etc. and combine the pasta and vegetables, this sauce is a perfect accompaniment for a light, pleasant, vegetarian supper.

The sauce will last for a week in a coolish kitchen, longer in a fridge.

METHOD

Blend together the garlic, red pepper or pimento, Hoi Sin, vinegar. Then add, mayonnaise fashion, the olive oil and last of all the coriander.

Hoi Sin sauce, mostly available in Oriental groceries is nowadays common on the "Oriental" shelves of large supermarkets. It often is called Chinese Barbecue Sauce, with Hoi Sin, in parenthesis, beneath.

Coriander

MEAT

Meat perfectly cooked – whether grilled or roasted, is often enhanced by the presence of herbs. Think of a few blades of rosemary on a leg of lamb, or a sprinkling of thyme and black pepper on a simple roast beef. But, it's in the recipes made using the slightly more demanding materials – liver, sausage meat, mince, that the choices of seasoning really come into their own.

Thyme

Rosemary

Minced Venison or Lean Minced Beef in a Piquant Sauce

INGREDIENTS:

450 gm of minced venison (1 lb)
1 small onion
1 egg
2 slices of brown bread, soaked in a little water, then wrung out
1 tablespoon of parsley
1 teaspoon of allspice
A pinch of Oriental five-spice powder
1 (scant) teaspoon of salt
1/2 teaspoon of black pepper
2 tablespoons of wine vinegar (3 Am. tablespoons)
1 heaped tablespoon of brown sugar (2 Am. tablespoons)
120 ml of tomato passata (4 fl.oz : 1/2 Am. cup)
120 ml of beef stock (4 fl.oz : 1/2 Am. cup)
2 gherkins finely minced
2 pickled walnuts, finely minced
1 red or yellow pepper, de-seeded, de -cored and finely minced
The grated zest of 1 orange
2 teaspoons of soy sauce
1 small chilli, de-seeded, de-ribbed and very finely minced
1 tablespoon of parsley

You need the leanest possible meat for these meatballs, which is why I recommend minced venison. Very, very lean beef, finely minced, will do as well, but fat is really The Enemy in this particular dish. A pound of meat will feed five or six people amply. Served with rice, mashed or boiled potatoes, and several vegetables, this will give you an economical feast.

METHOD

First make the meatballs. Mix together the meat with the onion, egg, washed and wrung out bread, parsley, allspice, five-spice powder and the salt and pepper. You can use a food processor for this if you have one, otherwise, mix it together very, very thoroughly.

Lightly oil a roasting tin, and form little meat balls, which you place in the tin. Cover the tin with aluminium foil, and roast the meatballs in a medium oven. Heat up the wine vinegar. Add the brown sugar, and bring it to the boil. Then add the tomato passata and the stock and the rest of the other ingredients. When the mixture has come to a boil, reduce to a simmer, and cook for ten minutes.

By this time, the meatballs should be ready. Add them and all of their juices to the sauce. Simmer for another ten minutes. If the mixture is too reduced, you can add a little water.

A delicious and spicy meal!

Lamb Noisette with Lavender and Mustard

INGREDIENTS:

1 whole noisette of lamb

1 clove of garlic

1 shallot

3 slices of white bread, chopped into breadcrumbs

1 level teaspoon of lavender

1 (level) tablespoon of Dijon mustard (Am. heaped)

Salt and pepper

A very little mild cooking oil (sunflower oil)

A whole noisette will feed four or five people amply. It is a longish sort of rolled fillet of lamb, bound together and covered by a thin layer of fat. To cook it, you will probably have to cut it into two or three pieces, in order to first fit it into a frying pan, then into the oven. Tender, with a splendid flavour, this particular cut is best served nice and pink – but if that isn't to your own particular taste, you can cook it for another five minutes or so.

METHOD

Preheat your oven to its hottest roasting temperature. While you are doing this, heat a heavy bottomed frying pan, and brush it very, very lightly with a little cooking oil. Now brown the noisette on all sides (as I said, you'll probably have to cut it once or twice). When it is browned, remove from the frying pan, and place it in a roasting tin. Chop the shallot and garlic very finely, and mix them into the breadcrumbs with the mustard and lavender. It should be a thickish paste. Pat this onto the top and sides of the noisette. Roast it at the highest temperature for ten to fifteen minutes, (depending upon the heat of your oven), then turn off the heat and allow to sit for another quarter of an hour. Slice it in inch thick chunks onto heated plates, placing a sliver of cooked savoury crust with every portion. Serve with mashed potatoes and a few green vegetables.

Lavender

Lamb's Liver with Thyme, Balsamic Vinegar, Marsala and Basil

INGREDIENTS:

80 gm of lamb's liver per
person, finely sliced
(3 – 4 oz)

A few slivers of finely
sliced onion

1/2 teaspoon of thyme

1 – 2 teaspoons of olive oil

15 ml of Balsamic vinegar
(1/2 fl.oz : 1 Am.
tablespoon)

30 ml of Marsala
(1 fl.oz : 2 Am. tablespoons)

2 leaves of basil per
serving, finely shredded

A little milk

Seasoned flour
(salt and pepper)

Lamb's liver is delicious, nutritious and cheap – it's a wonder that it isn't more popular. It's also astonishingly quick to prepare – make sure that you have all the ingredients on hand, before you start, as this is one of the most instant meals I know. Of course, you must have all the other elements of the meal ready to serve, before you even start!

METHOD

This takes very, very little time, so have all your ingredients at the ready. Heat a heavy bottomed frying pan, and add the oil. Then add the onion slivers, and when they start to change colour, dip the liver slices into the milk, then into the flour, dredging them thoroughly, but lightly. Add them to the hot onions, and when they are brown on one side, turn them. Add the thyme. Now add the Balsamic vinegar. When that just starts to bubble, add the Marsala. The vinegar and Marsala will amalgamate into a sauce. Turn off the heat and allow the meat to rest (it continues to cook for a minute longer), then serve, garnished with the shredded basil leaves.

Thyme

Stuffed Beafsteak Tomatoes or Large Mushrooms

INGREDIENTS:

Either 6 very large
beefsteak tomatoes or
6 very large mushrooms

The Rosemary Tomato
Sauce

1 lb of sausage meat
(the best you can find)

2 slices of bread,
brown or white
or a bread roll,
soaked in a little water,
then drained out and
squeezed

3 cloves of garlic

1 small onion or
half a large onion

1 teaspoon of fennel seeds
or a handful of
fresh fennel leaves

1 handful of parsley

1 teaspoon of dried
oregano

A (scant) teaspoon of salt

A (scant) teaspoon of
black pepper

When my husband and I were young and poor in Paris, years ago, we used to frequent a restaurant on the Rue du Dragon, on the Left Bank It had two elderly, fierce dragonesses as proprietors and was famous for its succulent stuffed tomatoes, cheap enough for our occasional treats.

Memories of that dish drove me to make my own, when I fed a large family on not very much money. The same recipe was later used to stuff large mushrooms. Large field mushrooms, gathered in the autumn, are the first choice. But, any other very, very large mushrooms available will do nicely.

For this recipe, you'll need the Rosemary Tomato Sauce which is in another part of this book.

METHOD

Oil the bottom of a roasting dish, pyrex dish or casserole large enough to stand the mushrooms or tomatoes in.

If you are using the tomatoes, cut off the top of the tomatoes in such a way that they can be put back onto the filled tomatoes in order to form lids. Scoop out the middle of the tomatoes – that is the ribs, seeds and the watery liquid. Discard the seeds and as much of the watery liquid as you can, but add whatever is left to the filling.

If you are using the mushrooms, cut off their stalks and add these to the rest of the filling.

Coat the cooking dish or casserole with a teaspoon or two of the Rosemary Tomato

INGREDIENTS CONTINUED:

A few drops of Tabasco or a sprinkling of cayenne

1 egg; a little oil (Olive if possible)

A few breadcrumbs and parsley for a garnish

Sauce, then stand the mushrooms or tomatoes in it, ready to receive their filling.

In a food processor, combine the onion, garlic, herbs and egg. Add the bread, then the sausage meat, and finally the leftover bits of either tomato or mushrooms.

Pile this mixture into the tomatoes or mushrooms. In the case of the tomatoes, replace the tops. Spoon on some of the Rosemary Tomato Sauce, about a tablespoon, more or less, per mushroom or tomato. Scatter with a few breadcrumbs, then a little trickle of oil. Cover the casserole tightly with aluminum foil, and bake it in a medium oven for forty to forty-five minutes. Dust well with parsley before serving, and be sure to spoon the juices in the bottom of the casserole over each serving.

Oregano

POULTRY

I have only given a few recipes for these, though they are some of the most popular with my family.

It is possible to substitute turkey breast for chicken breast, in most recipes. If a recipe calls for strips of chicken, then strips of filleted turkey breast can be substituted – or, if available, the filleted saddles of rabbit, tame or wild. And, most recipes which call for a whole chicken can be adapted to rabbit. If the rabbit is wild, about ten minutes more cooking may be called for.

Chicken Breasts with Basil, Sherry Vinegar and Cream

INGREDIENTS:

150 gm of chicken breast per serving (6 – 8 oz), skinned, off the bone, and cut into three or four thickish strips. In other words, either a smallish breast cut up, or half of a large chicken breast;

30ml of sherry vinegar (1fl.oz : 2 Am. tablespoons)

A few finely chopped shreds of red onion

A small amount of sunflower oil

60 ml of dry white wine (2 fl.oz : 4 Am. tablespoons)

A generous handful of chopped fresh basil

Salt and pepper

Small amount of cream (scant tablespoon)

More shredded basil for a garnish

An easy and quick supper dish. Good with plain rice or a baked potato to mop up the sauce. To do it, you must have all the ingredients ready and at hand.

METHOD

Heat up a heavy bottomed frying pan, and brush it with the oil. Stir fry the chicken strips until they start to brown, with the few shreds of onion. Add the salt and pepper. Next, add the sherry vinegar and the white wine, turning the chicken strips until they feel solid rather than floppy. Turn down the heat a little, and add the basil and cream. Cook until the strips of chicken are firm and when pierced, yield a yellow rather than red juice. This is only a matter of minutes. Turn onto a hot plate, and garnish with yet more shredded basil.

Basil

Haitian Chicken

INGREDIENTS:

1 chicken cut into serving sized joints

2 cloves of garlic, crushed

1 shallot or small onion, finely chopped

1 teaspoon of tomato puree

A handful of chopped parsley

Salt and pepper

The juice of 2 limes

A little light oil (sunflower or grapeseed)

I suppose that this is my own favourite recipe for chicken because it was one of the only slightly exotic things made for me as a small child; it was a regular feature of family meals.

It must be marinated overnight to taste right. Even though it seems a simple dish, a little planning must go into it.

It's best served with rice, plain or pilaff style. If you do a pilaff, stir in a few peas, a little chopped pimento and some kernels of corn which with this particular dish is perfection.

METHOD

Simplicity itself. Place the chicken bits in a glass bowl. Make a marinade with the garlic, onion or shallot; tomato puree; parsley and lime juice. Rub this onto the pieces of chicken, cover well and refrigerate overnight.

An hour before mealtime, remove the chicken from the marinade carefully saving the juices. Heat up a little oil in a large frying pan, and, after wiping dry the joints lightly, brown them in the hot fat. Place them in an ovenproof casserole. Discard the fat in the frying pan, and use it to briefly heat up the marinade. Pour this (there won't be very much at all) over the chicken. Add salt and pepper and cover the dish. Cook in a moderate oven for thirty-five to forty minutes. When you remove it from the oven, allow it a few minutes to "settle" before serving.

This is also wonderful, cold, as a salad.

Sauteed Chicken Livers with Sage and Fennel Seeds, Wrapped in Bacon

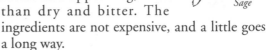
Sage

INGREDIENTS:

450 gm of chicken livers
(1 lb)

1 rasher of lean bacon
(smoked or unsmoked,
according to preference)
per liver – approximately
450 gm (1 lb)

1 (scant) tablespoon of
fennel seeds

6 fresh sage leaves,
very finely minced

3 tablespoons of soft
breadcrumbs

3 tablespoons of Parmesan
cheese, grated

A dash of salt

A good grating of freshly
milled black pepper

3 tablespoons of olive oil

3 – 4 fl.oz of sherry
(a little glass), any sort

toothpicks

This recipe will make even those who are slightly lukewarm about liver reconsider. There are enough tastes to tempt, and the texture of the finished dish is moist and appetising, rather than dry and bitter. The ingredients are not expensive, and a little goes a long way.

METHOD

Mix together the fennel seeds, minced sage leaves, breadcrumbs and parmesan. Season, very lightly with salt, more strength with pepper. Roll each chicken liver in this mixture, coating well, and then roll each chicken liver up in a rasher of bacon, covering it as much as possible and securing it with a toothpick. When this is finished you should have something between eight and ten little bundles, safely skewered.

Now, in a large frying pan, heat up the olive oil, and then brown these parcels. You will have to turn them about from time to time. It should take approximately ten minutes. Then, if there is an excess of oil in the pan (there shouldn't be, but from time to time bacon is not what it ought to be), discard most of this. Now, add the sherry and cook for another few minutes until there is a little bit of sticky, shiny sauce. Serve at once, but remove the toothpicks first, or warn your guests.

Chicken Legs, stuffed with Mushrooms, casseroled in an Onion and Balsamic Vinegar Sauce

INGREDIENTS:
SERVES 4

4 chicken thighs, boned and skinned if preferred (optional – a few sheets of caul fat)

70 gm of mushrooms (2 – 3 oz)

A small amount of olive oil, for brushing the bottom of a frying pan

1/2 teaspoon of thyme, salt, pepper

FOR THE SAUCE

1 (scant) kilo of onions, sliced thinly (2 lbs)

1 tablespoon of olive oil

1 teaspoon of salt

60 cl of red wine vinegar (2 fl.oz : 4 Am. tablespoons)

2 tablespoons of Balsamic vinegar

2 (scant) tablespoons of sugar

Chopped parsley and finely shredded basil

This recipe is a combination of several. The technique for cooking onions is one taught me by a Polish friend; Slavs are renowned for making great soups out of very, very few simple ingredients, and the slow cooking of the onions is the reason.

The actual recipe was originally for rabbit, which can be substituted but the stuffed thigh and chicken leg provide a good flavour without the bones ever present in casseroled rabbit.

I remove the skin from the chicken before boning it, as I don't like to eat all that fat. Instead, when boned and stuffed, I wrap each chicken portion in a little caul fat (also known as 'veil fat'). But the skin can be left on the chicken and each piece stuffed, wrapped and then fastened with a few toothpicks or skewers, which can be removed immediately before serving.

This recipe calls for three hours of cooking. Except for slicing up the onions and the boning of the chicken legs (which can nowadays often be bought, ready prepared), very little real time is spent at the stove. So this is ideal for occasions when the cook wants to spend as much time as possible away from the kitchen.

METHOD

For the chicken stuffing, chop the mushrooms finely and saute them in a lightly oiled pan, until the have disgorged then re-absorbed their fluid. Sprinkle with thyme, salt and pepper, cook for a minute longer, and then remove from the heat and allow them to cool.

Three hours before mealtime, cut the onions finely and place them in a heavy bottomed large saucepan. Put them on a medium heat, and stir them from time to time, until they have started to change their appearance from opaque to transparent. Don't put any fat in the pan and keep an eye on them lest they burn. When they are mostly transparent, add the tablespoon of olive oil, a teaspoon of salt and mix well. Cover the saucepan, lower the heat as much as you can and leave it to cook for an hour and a half. Occasionally check to see they aren't sticking – give them a stir or two. If the heat is low enough and the casserole heavy bottomed, this shouldn't be a problem.

At the end of an hour and a half, remove the cover and add the sugar. Turn up the heat, stirring, and continue to cook until the sugar has absorbed and the onions are completely caramelized and starting to brown. Then add the red wine vinegar.

Lower the heat briefly, and open out the previously boned chicken, dividing the cooled mushrooms between the pieces. Roll them up and either wrap them in caul fat or secure them together with a toothpick or skewer of some sort. Then, in a separate frying pan, brown the chicken legs. You shouldn't need any additional fat for this – for they are either wrapped in caul fat or are in their own skins. When they are nicely brown, on each side, add them to the caramelized onions, mixing them in well. Add a little salt and pepper and cover the casserole up. Then cook for forty minutes, either on top of the stove, over a very, very low flame, or in a slowish oven.

A quarter of an hour before serving, spoon out and discard any fatty excess floating at the top. Then add, for that last fifteen minutes, the two tablespoons of Balsamic vinegar and a vigorous sprinkling of freshly milled black pepper.

Garnish with chopped parsley and finely shredded fresh basil. For all the simplicity of its ingredients, this dish tastes sumptuous!

Pigeon Breasts with Port, Wine and Cream

INGREDIENTS:
SERVES 4

4 pairs of pigeon breasts

Half a small onion cut into fine slivers (not minced)

A small amount of oil, lard, duck fat or butter (to thinly coat the bottom of a hot frying pan)

150 ml of port (doesn't need to be 'vintage') (4 fl.oz : 1 cup)

150 ml of red wine (4 – 5 fl.oz : 1 cup)

Salt and pepper

Thyme

75 ml of cream (whipping or double) (2 – 3 fl.oz : $^1/_2$ cup)

Parsley

A teaspoon of green peppercorns (the liquid sort, soaked in brine, then drained before use)

If you have a ready supply of wood pigeon, this is a simple treat. Don't even bother to draw and pluck the birds, simply carve out the meat from the breasts. This is easy enough and will save much time and effort as there's very little else worth eating on the bird in the first place.

Traditionally, diners were served three breasts each, but time and experience have shown that this too much, for even the most copious appetite, These little morsels are very dense in texture as well as intense in flavour. It is advisable, after cooking and just before serving, to slice them finely into a fan or small slivers – so make sure you have a very sharp fine knife for this. Serving them on either a crouton or piece of toast to soak up all of their juices is a good idea as well.

You will also need a larger frying pan then you might at first think, if you are cooking four pairs of pigeon breasts. If the breasts are crowded into a small pan, the sauce doesn't seem to emulsify quickly enough.

METHOD

Heat up the large frying pan, and then brush it with a little fat, coating the pan lightly and evenly. Then sear the pigeon breasts, browning them well on each side. Salt them, then pepper and a generous dusting with thyme, then add the onion slivers. Continue to cook for a minute. Then stand well back before adding the port. This should burst into an alcoholic and glorious flame, so don't hover too closely over it or you'll lose your eyebrows. When the flames have finished add the red wine. Turn the breasts over as you cook them. Then add the peppercorns (approximately two or three per serving). When the juices have started to reduce, and there is a slightly glazed appearance, add the cream, stirring it well. Leave it to cook for another minute, or until the sauce has thickened and is brown and glossy. Now, turn the heat off altogether and leave it alone for five minutes.

You must allow this dish to 'rest.' The meat will continue to cook but the tissues 'relax' becoming tender.

Last of all, finely slice the breasts, cutting them on the 'cross', if possible. Spoon them onto croutons or toast on hot plates, scraping all the sauce onto them. Dust well with parsley.

Stay-up-late Turkey – or Simplify Christmas!

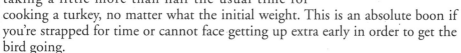

This is probably the most useful recipe in the book! It has the advantage of only taking a little more than half the usual time for cooking a turkey, no matter what the initial weight. This is an absolute boon if you're strapped for time or cannot face getting up extra early in order to get the bird going.

It does have a few drawbacks. The appearance of the roasted bird, minus its legs, does take getting used to. And it does mean a half hour of concentration, the day before you cook the meal, in order to bone out the legs and make your stuffing.

But, like most poultry, the actual character of the two types of meat – white and dark – are so different, white meat needing only a simple, perfunctory roasting till done, the dark meat requiring longer and slower cooking, if on the bone. Usually as cooks, we sacrifice one of them for the other. Either the white breast meat is juicy and the dark legs tough, or the dark meat is succulent and the white meat is dried out.

Cooking the white meat on the bone ensures that it remains juicy, and even if the prospect of deboning and removing the tendons of both legs seems daunting to contemplate, it is neither difficult nor messy, just a bit fiddly.

So, to start – cut off the leg and thigh of the bird at the top, moving it about with your hands in order to find the little bit of tendon where the thigh is connected to the main carcass. When you reach the join of the thigh with the rest of the body, twist the leg and you'll see just where to slice.

Then, at the top of the thigh, remove the flesh from the top of the thigh bone by scraping away at it fairly gently, with a smallish sharp knife. You should be able to ease it round the corner, elbowy sort of joint, but all along the lower, leg part of the bird are several tendons. These are like long strips of plastic with triangular ends, attached either to the bottom bit of the turkey leg or the top end of the joint. Scrape away as much meat as you can from them, and if you are worried about this, you can cut a slit all along the length of the leg and thigh. You should be left with a thick, flattish strip of turkey flesh covered with skin.

Reserve the turkey leg bones, tendons, gizzard and neck, for your stock and gravy.

Once you've boned out both turkey legs, place one skin side down. Cover it with your stuffing, then cover that with the other boned leg, skin side up. Using

INGREDIENTS: STUFFING

225 gm of breadcrumbs
(¹/₂lb)

450 gm of lean
sausagemeat (1 lb)
(I use venison sausage)

1 medium onion (¹/₂ lb)
cut finely and sauteed
gently in a little oil until
soft

1 teaspoon of dried
lavender

60 gm of chopped walnuts
or pecans (2 oz)

60 gm of prunes (stoned)
or apricots (2 oz),
cut finely

Dash of cayenne and a turn
or two of freshly ground
black pepper

The turkey liver,
finely minced

1 egg, beaten with
60 ml of sherry (2 fl.oz)
and 60 ml of port (2 fl.oz)

either a few large rubber bands or some string, fashion this into a sort of "joint" which can be placed in a smallish roasting pan, to be cooked in the oven, separately from the main bit of turkey.

Cover the main turkey carcass with a mixture of Dijon mustard and sunflower oil, and stuff a cut orange in the cavity. If there is extra fat in the cavity, remove it and save for the gravy. Cover it lightly with a bit of foil and roast it, twenty minutes to the pound, until done. First in the high oven, then, after twenty minutes in a medium to lowish oven. Forty minutes before serving, remove the foil so that the bird browns nicely on top.

Ten minutes after you've started roasting the main bit of the bird, start roasting the leg-and-stuffing joint. Remove both of the bits of the turkey at least a quarter of an hour before serving, in order to allow the meat to "rest". This should make slicing and serving easy. The stuffing "joint" should seem like a rather juicy, succulent hot galantine and the dark meat will be tender and tendon free.

Stuffing

METHOD

Mix these all together until they are a sticky clump. Place on one of the spread out boned legs, cover with the other and bind together to make a sort of "joint". Roast for slightly less time than the main bit of the turkey.

Stay-up-late Turkey – Gravy

INGREDIENTS: GRAVY

Any lumps of turkey fat

The neck, bones, sinews, gizzard and heart of the bird

1 chopped carrot

1 chopped onion

1 stick of celery, chopped

Handful of parsley

2 bay leaves

A dash or two of thyme

1 tablespoon of soy sauce

2 tablespoons of sweet sherry

METHOD

In a heavy bottomed saucepan, melt and render down the turkey fat. Place the bones, sinews and bits of the turkey in the hot fat, and stirring well, brown them all thoroughly. Then add the onion, carrot and celery and stir them, to cook briefly. Cover well with water with at least an inch to spare, and bring it up to the boil. Then add the parsley, bay and thyme and leave to simmer until you're about to leave the bird to brown. Then remove the saucepan from the heat and strain it out. Leave it in a bowl or saucepan, plunged into a basin or bowl of cold water, so that it cools rapidly. Then spoon or skim off the fat from the top. If it is cool enough, this should be easy, but if not, it can be skimmed off with several wipes around the top with a crumpled paper towel or two.

Warm up the defatted liquid and add the soy sauce and sweet sherry. When the turkey is finished cooking, add the juices which have come off the bird to the liquid. If you like the gravy thickened, add a couple of teaspoons of cornflour, dissolved and stirred in a little water. Boil the liquid rapidly, just before serving.

VEGETARIAN IDEAS

This sounds like a bit of an isolation unit, when it really is a few suggestions for the sorts of meal which are popular, easy and not very expensive. All of these recipes are the sorts of food which have been most popular with growing children and their friends, making instant entertaining affordable. They have also been the most successful recipes for staff meals in our restaurant. People who work continuously with food often seem to prefer this sort of food on a day-to-day basis! I'm also including a couple of diagrams for that little present-day mystery: the wrapping of filo parcels.

Green Herb Sauce for Spaghetti
with a few variations

INGREDIENTS:

2 handfuls of parsley, stalks removed

A small handful of thyme, de-stalked

A handful of marjoram, with the woody stem removed

2 cloves of garlic

1 shallot

Salt and pepper

Cayenne

Olive oil

OPTIONAL:

A handful of basil or the finely chopped green leaves off of a branch of fresh rosemary; or the flowers of 2 or 3 fresh lavender plants.

The easiest sauce in the world, if you have a garden, this green dressing for pasta is an answer to what to prepare when there are unexpected guests for tea or supper, and there is nothing more than a package or two of dried pasta on hand.

METHOD

For this, you need either a food processor or blender – and all you do is to mix the garlic, shallot, and green ingredients together, whizz to chop them, and dribble in enough olive oil to cover them. Salt and pepper to taste.

This can be used as is for spaghetti, with or without parmesan or grated cheese. Either the basil or rosemary or lavender can be added – but not all together!

You can also toast a few sesame seeds (by placing them in a hot, dry frying pan for a minute or two), or sunflower seeds, or pine kernels (pine nuts). But these aren't strictly essential, just another welcome variation.

The secret is in preparing it at the last minute, from fresh ingredients. Freshness is all.

Marjoram

Rosemary Tomato Sauce for Macaroni or Pizza

INGREDIENTS:

1 tablespoon of olive oil

1 medium onion, chopped

1 blade of celery,
finely minced

1 carrot, grated

1 clove of garlic,
finely chopped

5 large beefsteak tomatoes,
peeled and de-seeded
or a 400 gm (14 oz) tin of
plum or chopped tomatoes

1 teaspoon of sugar

1 teaspoon of tomato puree

2 bay leaves

A handful of chopped
parsley

A branch of rosemary

Salt and pepper

A standby sauce, this can be used either simply with pasta and grated cheese, or as a pizza sauce, or together with a bechamel (cheese sauce) between layers of pasta, as in a lasagne.

METHOD

Heat up the oil and then gently fry the onion in it until the onion starts to go transparent. Then add the celery, carrot and garlic, and continue to cook, stirring, for another couple of minutes. Last of all, add the tomatoes (or tinned tomatoes), sugar and tomato puree, and stir them well in. Add the herbs and then enough water to cover the sauce for about a half inch. Bring it to the boil, then reduce it to a simmer. Leave it to reduce, uncovered, for a half hour. Then remove the bay leaf and rosemary branch, and add salt and pepper to taste.

This sauce can be finely chopped, if you want a smooth sauce, or served as is. The vegetables and herbs flavour it well, so that it can be used quite sparingly.

Stored covered, in a refrigerator, this sauce will last up to six days. And, frozen in smallish batches, it is very useful indeed.

Bay

Filo Parcels of Leeks with Basil and Ricotta, with Tomato Basil Vinaigrette

INGREDIENTS: FOR 4 PARCELS

4 sheets of filo pastry

1 leek, very finely chopped (use as much of the green as you can)

A teacup of ricotta cheese

A good handful of finely shredded basil

Salt and pepper

A little olive oil to saute the leek

A little olive oil for brushing the filo with

Filo pastry, now widely available, is a neat light way of dressing up simple and homely ingredients. It can be wrapped, in neat triangular parcels, around a piece of uncooked fish, which has been seasoned with salt, pepper, and has a little parsley or chervil sprinkled on it. The wrapping of it, simply done by turning up a triangle and then continuing to fold on, looks for complicated than it is. But a filo parcel can also be made by turning in the ends of the pastry and then rolling it round. *(Diagram on page 47)*.

The pastry must be lightly oiled and folded in half, no matter which way it is wrapped. I find it easiest to brush the pastry with a little olive oil, rather than melted butter.

In any case, the filo and its contents are both perfectly cooked when the pastry itself is brown. To do this, place the pastry on a tray and bake in as hot an oven as you can summon up. When done, the temperature of the oven can be lowered and the pastry "held" for another five or ten minutes.

Here is a vegetarian filling for filo parcels which is light, tasty and easy to prepare.

METHOD

Chop the leek very finely and saute it in the olive oil until it is quite soft. Then combine it with the ricotta and the shredded basil. Salt and pepper to taste. Allow this to cool thoroughly.

Then, divide it into four portions. Place on the oiled filo pastry and either roll or fold it up

INGREDIENTS: VINAIGRETTE

1 tablespoon of
red wine vinegar

1 teaspoon of
Balsamic vinegar

1 clove of garlic

1 shallot

1 tablespoon of sun-dried
tomatoes which have
been stored in oil

1 tablespoon of
tomato passata

2 handfuls of fresh basil

Salt and pepper

240cc of olive oil
(8 fl.oz : 1 cup)

into oblong or triangular parcels. They can be chilled until you're ready to use them, and then can be baked in a very hot oven, for ten to fifteen minutes.

I like to serve them with the following vinaigrette:

Vinaigrette

METHOD

Combine the vinegar, tomatoes, shallot, garlic and basil. Whizz or blend. Then dribble in the olive oil and correct the seasoning with salt and pepper.

Serve the filos accompanied by the vinaigrette, garnished with finely shredded basil.

A treat.

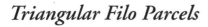

Triangular Filo Parcels

Sheet of Filo Pastry

1. Oil the bottom half (brush it with olive oil OR melted butter).

2. Fold the top half over, then brush the other half with oil.

3. Place the filling where the "X" is.

4. Fold the bottom right corner into a triangle (along the dotted line shown) covering the filling. Then fold over the corner again

5. Fold again from top right hand corner. Then fold along the dotted line.

6. Wrap over what is left on itself and you should be left with a triangle, which is your finished, wrapped filo.

   Place this on your baking sheet!

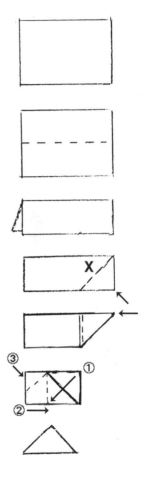

Filo Rectangles

Sheet of Filo Pastry

1. Oil the bottom half (brush with olive oil OR melted butter

2. Fold the top half over; then brush the other half with oil.

3. Place the filling to the right in the middle.

4. Fold the top and bottom edges over the filling.

5. Fold the parcel over and over, so that you're left with a wrapped rectangle.

   Place this on your baking sheet.

Rice and Vermicelli Pilaff cooked in a Vegetable Stock

This is one recipe made by volume only. So that whatever the size of your cup – whether a teacup, coffee cup, or mug, you must measure all ingredients with the same receptacle.

You can use a vegetable stock cube for this. Just add a scant teaspoon of thyme to it. But, if you are interested in making a pleasant vegetable stock, for this recipe, here is a suggestion:

METHOD
In a little vegetable oil, brown slightly an onion; carrot; blade of celery; half leek; two or three mushrooms. Cover them with three inches of water, a bay leaf, teaspoon of thyme and a few parsley stalks and bring to the boil. reduce to a simmer, cover and cook gently for a half hour. Then strain the stock out, and add two teaspoons of soy sauce and a teaspoon of tomato puree. Salt and pepper to taste.

INGREDIENTS: PILAFF

1 tablespoon of olive oil
1 tablespoon of butter
1 cup of vermicelli (very thin spaghetti), well broken up
1 cup of rice
2 shallots, finely chopped
3 cups of vegetable stock, brought to the boil.

This pilaff, brown and savoury, is either a wonderful accompaniment to a main dish (it's terrific with the Chicken Legs in the Onion and Balsamic sauce). But it's also a crowd pleaser, especially if there are vegetarians present.

METHOD
In a heavy bottomed saucepan, melt the butter and then add the olive oil. Stir in the shallots and vermicelli and keep stirring until all the grains are coated. Then add the rice (long grain or Basmati are probably best, here), and continue to stir over the heat, until all the rice is also lightly coated. Then add the boiling vegetable stock, stir briefly – very briefly, and cover the saucepan tightly. Reduce the heat, and cook it for twenty minutes. Last of all, remove the lid of the saucepan, and place a cloth on it, and then put the lid back. Leave the saucepan off of the heat for at least ten minutes, so that all the remaining steam within is absorbed by the contents, before serving.

Norfolk Lavender, Lavender and Other Herbs and You

Norfolk Lavender is England's only large scale lavender farm. A family firm, we grow almost 100 acres of lavender, as well as other herbs, principally rosemary. Most of our lavender is distilled to extract oil for perfumery or aromatherapy uses. For many years the flowers have also been dried for pot pourri and sachets; and now, more recently, for culinary purposes too.

At Caley Mill, our 19th century headquarters, we laid out our herb garden on the lines of a medieval monastery physick garden: that is small individual beds so that each herb could be grown separately and then harvested for use in medicines. In your own garden, many interesting plantings like the Tudor knot garden can be made.

For the cook, of course, the ideal is to have a herb bed as near as possible to your kitchen door. Then, you can nip out with your scissors and harvest your herbs at their freshest.

When growing your herbs, choose a sunny spot with light, well-drained, sandy soil. For those not lucky enough to have a garden, many

The physick garden

herbs will grow extremely well in pots on your kitchen window cill or in a window box – decorative, fragrant and useful. Parsley, basil, thyme, sage, mint, savory and chives can be grown in 3 in. (7 cm) or 5 in. (12 cm) pots. The larger herbs, like lavender and rosemary will need a 10 in. (25 cm) pot eventually. All are best planted with a little "crock" at the bottom of the pot; then use a good general compost (preferably peat-free), or loam, with an additional $1/3$ of sharp sand, mixing it well. The square stemmed fragrant herbs like mint, thyme, marjoram, lavender and rosemary need little water. The more fleshy herbs like parsley, dill and basil should be grown in slightly heavier compost and need slightly more water.

Most herbs are best used fresh. If you can't grow them at home, you can probably get them in your supermarket either fresh or freeze-dried, but these should be used up quite quickly. If you are growing your own herbs and want to keep some for later, you can try freezing or drying them. If freezing, experiment first to find out which ones work the best.

If you plan to dry your own lavender for cooking (or, incidentally, pot pourri) leave the bloom as long as possible, even if the flowers are beginning to brown, because the natural oils will then be at their best. In this way you get a double benefit; you can enjoy the colour of the flowers in the garden while they are in full bloom and also have the use of the harvest: but beware! Leave the lavender too long and the next August thunderstorm will knock the flowers off onto the ground and there will be nothing at all to collect. When you decide to harvest, cut the lavender and tie or rubberband the stalks into single hand-sized bunches. Hang them in a dark, warm, dry place with a sheet of newspaper underneath to catch any florets which drop. When the bunches are quite dry, simply rub the heads, the florets will separate quite easily: then you can bag up your harvest for use throughout the year.

If you are a dried flower arranger, you should pick the flowers just before the florets start to open; this ensures that the bloom will remain on the stalk and will not drop. (Don't forget to pick the stalks as long as possible). Then dry the bunches as described above.

Do not be inhibited by the idea that lavender is a scent. We think it is especially delicious, as Carla has said, when steaming fish; also in chutneys, lamb and inside a roasting chicken. Try a sprig of lavender leaves in a stew instead of rosemary or bay leaves.

Lavender is the herb of cleanliness and calm. Indeed, it has been said that some zoo keepers find it renders lions and tigers quite docile under its influence – try it on the family.

LAVENDER RECIPES

Lavender items are served in our Norfolk Lavender Tearoom. All our dishes are prepared and cooked in our own kitchen, where an inventive and enthusiastic team have introduced many excellent recipes using lavender. They are extremely popular with our customers and we now share the following ones with you our readers.

Lavender Tea

Add two or three flower heads of dried lavender to your favourite tea in your favourite tea caddy. This will impart a delicious little "extra" to your brew.

Lavender

Lavender Sorbet

INGREDIENTS:

2 ripe Ogen melons

The juice of 2 lemons

120 gm of caster sugar (4 oz)

15 gm lavender flowers (fresh or dried) ($^1/_2$ oz)

2 egg whites

$^1/_2$ bottle of dry sparkling wine or champagne

METHOD

Liquidise the melons, lemon juice and castor sugar. Infuse the lavender flowers for twelve minutes only in sparkling wine which has been gently warmed. Drain and press through a sieve. Add this liquid to the puree followed by the egg whites. Add a drop or so of blue vegetable colouring and put in an ice-cream machine until done, or whisk the mixture together and freeze, whisking every twenty minutes until set.

Lavender Maids of Honour

INGREDIENTS:

180 gm of short pastry (6 oz)

Jam

60 gm of margarine (2 oz)

60 gm of caster sugar (2 oz)

60 gm of self-raising flour (2 oz)

1 egg

2 teaspoons of lavender heads

METHOD

Roll out the pastry and cut into twenty-four rounds and line your tins. Place a little jam in each pastry case, cream the margarine and sugar and fold in the beaten egg, flour and lavender heads. Place a teaspoon of mixture into each case and bake at 190°C – 200°C (375°F – 400°F) or gas mark 5 – 6 for twenty minutes.

Lavender Fairy Cakes

INGREDIENTS:

180 gm of self-raising flour (6 oz)

120 gm of margarine (4oz)

120 gm of sugar (4 oz)

3 eggs

4 teaspoons of lavender heads

METHOD

Cream the margarine and sugar and add the lightly beaten egg, flour and lavender heads. Place a teaspoon of the mixture into a baking case. Cook at 190°C (375°F) for fifteen minutes.

TOPPING

Decorate with butter icing.

180 gm of icing sugar

90 gm of margarine and a little lavender colouring

Lavender Chutney

INGREDIENTS:
MAKES 9 lb
or 18 ¹/₂ lb JARS

4 tablespoons of
mustard seed (5 Am)

---

12 lemons

---

12 medium onions

---

270 gm of sultanas
(8 oz)

---

3 cinnamon sticks

---

2 teaspoons of allspice

2.25 kg of granulated
sugar
(5 lb)

1700 ml of apple cider
vinegar (3¹/₄ pt)

---

2 cups of lavender heads

METHOD

Cut the lemon up into small pieces and cover over with vinegar. Leave to soak for twenty-four hours, sprinkle with salt.

Place the lemon, vinegar and all the other ingredients into a pan. Put the lavender heads into a muslin bag and hang in a saucepan. Simmer gently, stirring occasionally for about one and a half hours or until it thickens.

Lavender Marmalade

INGREDIENTS:

1 kg of Seville oranges
(2 lb 3 oz)

1 lemon

2000 ml of water (3³/4 pt)

2 kg of preserving sugar

35 gm of dried lavender
flowers tied in a muslin bag
(1 oz)
(Being so light, lavender is
awkward to weigh
accurately. A volume
measure is a good
alternative – if you tip the
flowers into a measuring
jug to the 200 ml line, that
will be about 35 gm)

METHOD

Cut the fruit in half, extract the juice and pips, shred the peel as you like it. If the pith is thick, remove some. Put the peel, juice and water into a pan, add pips in a muslin bag and bring to the boil. Simmer gently for approximately one and a half hours or until the peel is tender. Squeeze the bag of pips to release any liquid and remove. Stir in the warmed water over a gentle heat until dissolved. Add lavender in a muslin bag and bring to a fast boil for ten minutes. Press the juice from the lavender bag and remove. Continue a fast boil until setting point is reached. Leave to stand for a half hour, stir, turn into warm dry jars and cover to make airtight.

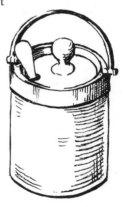

Lavender Jelly

INGREDIENTS:

2.5 kg of cooking apples
(6 lb)

2250 ml of water (5 pt)

2.5 kg of sugar (5 lb)

5 tablespoons of
lemon juice (7 Am.)

3 handfuls (approximately)
of lavender flowers
(or 3/4 large teacup)

METHOD

Wash the apples and chop them; peel core and all. Put them into a pan with the water and bring to the boil, simmer until pulpy – about thirty minutes. Pour into a jelly bag and leave overnight **without** disturbance.

The next day, measure the juice and add one pound of sugar to every pint of juice (800 gm per litre of juice). Place in a pan and bring to the boil with the lavender. Boil steadily for about twenty minutes until the setting point is reached. Skim off the surface scum and then stir in the lemon juice. Pour into warmed jars and cover.

Lavender Madeira Cake

INGREDIENTS:

150 gm of margarine (5 oz)

2 tablespoons of
lavender heads (2 1/2 Am.)

150 gm of caster sugar (5 oz)

3 eggs

30 gm of self-raising flour
(10 oz)

1/2 teaspoon of
lemon essence

METHOD

Cream the margarine and sugar and gradually add the lightly whisked eggs. Add the essence and lavender flower heads, fold in the flour.

Bake at 170°C – 180°C (325°F – 350°F) or gas mark 3 – 4 for one and a half hours. Decorate with lavender water icing if required or place lavender flowers on top.

Lavender Biscuits

INGREDIENTS:

240 gm of unsalted butter
(8 oz)

180 gm of margarine (6 oz)

60 gm of butter (2 oz)

120 gm of caster sugar (4 oz)

1 egg, lightly beaten

240 gm of self-raising flour
(8 oz)

4 teaspoons of dried
lavender flowers

METHOD

Cream the butter and sugar. Add the egg and beat in well. Mix in the flour and dried lavender flowers. Place a teaspoon of the mixture onto a baking tray lined with non-stick baking parchment. Bake at 180°C (350°F) for approximately ten to fifteen minutes or until the biscuits are pale golden in colour

Makes approximately 24 biscuits.

Lavender and Lemon Scones

INGREDIENTS:

450 gm of self-raising flour
(1 lb)

30 gm of caster sugar (1 oz)

90 gm of hard margarine
(3 oz)

2 eggs, beaten, save some
egg to glaze

A little milk

1 teaspoon of lemon juice

2 teaspoons of dried
lavender flower heads

METHOD

Mix the flour, sugar, lavender and margarine together until it resembles breadcrumbs. Add the milk and lemon juice to a beaten egg and gradually pour into the dry ingredients. Mix until all the flour is incorporated but the mixture is slightly sticky. Transfer to a floured board and knead gently. Roll out to approximately 18 mm (³/4 in) thickness and using a 6.5 cm (2¹/2 in) cutter, cut into rounds and place on a greased tray and brush with a beaten egg. Bake at 200°C (400°F) for approximately ten to twelve minutes or until well risen and golden in colour

Lavender and Lemon Sponge

INGREDIENTS:

150 gm of self raising flour
(5 oz)

90 gm of soft margarine
(3 oz)

90 gm of caster sugar
(3 oz)

1/2 level teaspoon of
baking powder

5 drops of lemon juice

1/4 cup of milk
(use as required)

2 beaten eggs

2 level teaspoons of
dried lavender flowers

You can follow this recipe or your own favourite sponge recipe will do – just add the dried lavender flowers.

METHOD

Using an electric mixer, cream the margarine and sugar until light and fluffy. Gradually add the eggs and a small amount of flour to prevent the mixture curdling. Gradually fold in the flour, dried lavender flowers and lemon juice. Divide the mixture between two greased and floured 7 in sandwich tins. Bake at 170°C (325°F – 350°F) for approximately ten to fifteen minutes. Leave to cool slightly in the tins before turning out onto a wire tray. Sandwich together with jam and lemon butter icing.

Lavender Shortbread

INGREDIENTS:

520 gm of plain flour
(1 lb 2 oz)

520 gm of soft margarine
(1 lb 2 oz)

240 gm of caster sugar
(8 oz)

240 gm of ground rice
(8 oz)

2 level teaspoons of dried lavender flowers

You can follow this recipe or your own favourite shortbread recipe will do – just add the dried lavender flowers.

METHOD

Using an electric mixer, place all the ingredients in the bowl. Begin mixing gradually. Switch to maximum speed only when all the ingredients are incorporated and the mixture leaves the sides of the bowl. Divide the mixture between five greased and floured 7 in sandwich tins. Bake at 160°C (310°F) for approximately thirty-five minutes. Cut each round into eight equal portions as soon as possible after leaving the oven. Leave to cool completely in the tins. Sprinkle with caster sugar.

Makes approximately 30.